The author and the illustrator are both gifted educators for the North Central Ohio Educational Service Center in Tiffin, Ohio. They team with a group of talented colleagues who have been instrumental in the creation of <u>My Child is Very Special</u>. Gifted services are not mandated in the state of Ohio, so this group has been tirelessly working together to increase awareness of the needs of our special students.

Sincere appreciation to our colleagues and dear friends Judy Back, Deb Kohler, Kim Bagent, Anne Kresser, Donna Bradley and Germaine Hines for the inspiration provided by their experience, knowledge, and creative efforts.

-DMK, dm

Thanks also to former English teacher and gifted education colleague, Judy Withrow for her complimentary editing.

N.L. Associates, Inc., 2003

All rights reserved. No part of this book may be reproduced in any manner whatever, including information storage or retrieval, in whole or in part (except for brief quotations in critical articles or reviews), without written permission from the publishers. For information, write to N.L. Associates, Inc., P.O. Box 1199, Hightstown, NJ 08520.

ISBN# 0-9721388

Printed in the United States

To my own three special children:
Kristy, Brian and David
-dm

mac :)

Dedicated to many special kids I love, especially Kelly and Mac
-DMK

Special Note: Mac, by the way, is the nickname for the illustrator of this book. She was a freelance artist and an art teacher before she began teaching gifted children. She shared with me that one of her lifelong goals was to illustrate a book and that is the main reason I wrote this book. When the process began I had no idea how timely this endeavor would be. This past year Mac was diagnosed with cancer and at the time of publication she began receiving home care through hospice.

-DMK

My child is very special,

said the mother to the nurse.

She'll never ride a bike;

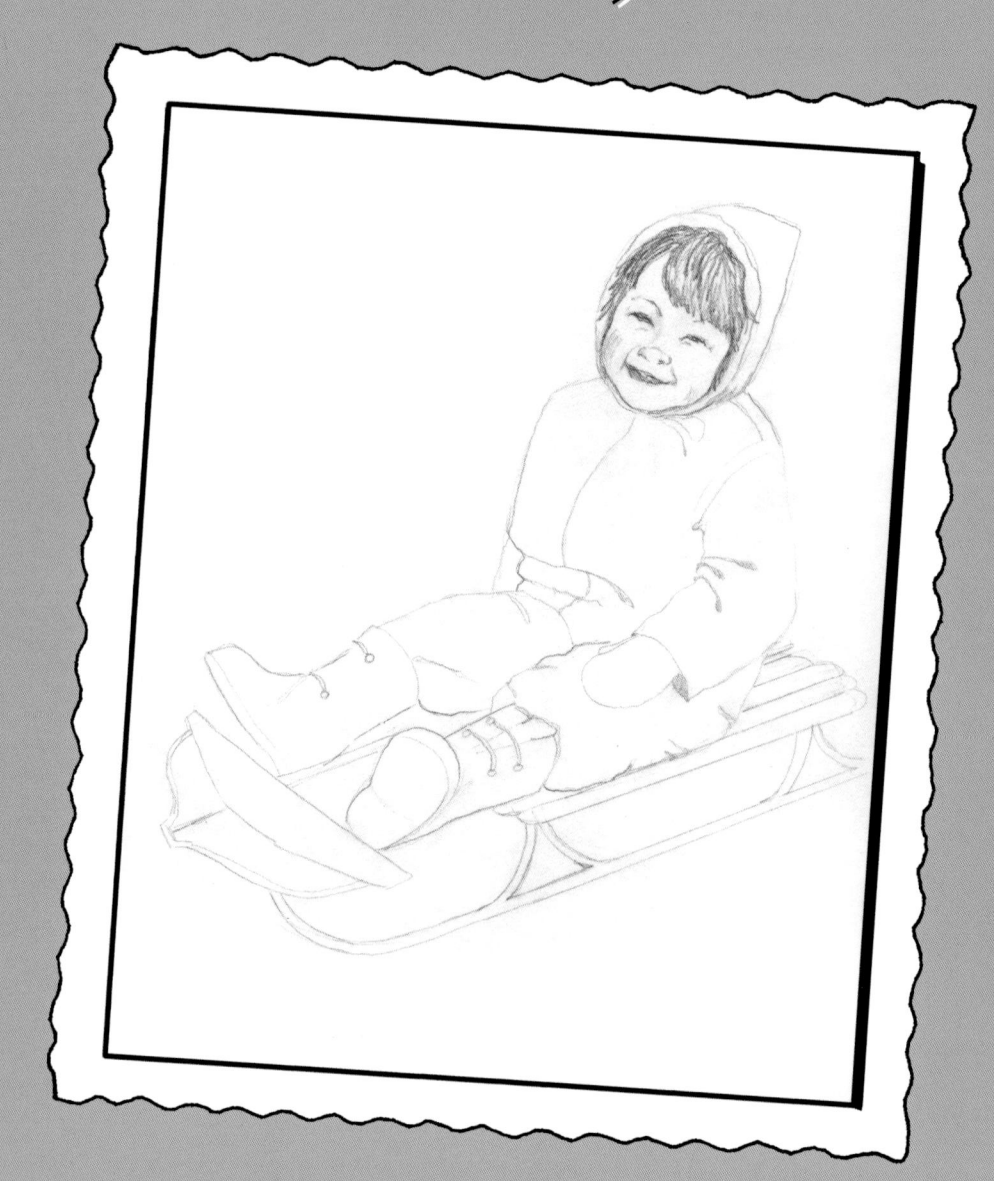

she'll never come in first.

She needs some special braces;

she needs some extra care.

Let's help her to succeed

and make the world aware.

My child is
   very special,

said the father
   to the coach.

His skills are well developed;

just look at his approach.

He needs to
be promoted

to reach his
full potential.

Give him extra playing time;

it really is essential.

Our child is very special,

said the parents at their school.

He has difficulty learning,

but he's really not a fool.

He needs to learn some special skills.

Please give him extra time.

Let's work on this together

so he doesn't fall behind.

My child is not special

just because she learns so fast.

It is okay to have her wait,

so she'll not outdo her class.

Please don't say that she is gifted

because others will complain

that she gets
    extra privileges

and I only
    want her fame.

Your child is very special,

the piano teacher said.

She learns with such perfection;

I've moved her way ahead.

She needs to be encouraged

to always do her best.

She needs to have a challenge

to find
complete success.

Your child is very special;

he draws with great detail.

Because he's only eight years old,

he surely will excel.

This talent is a blessing.

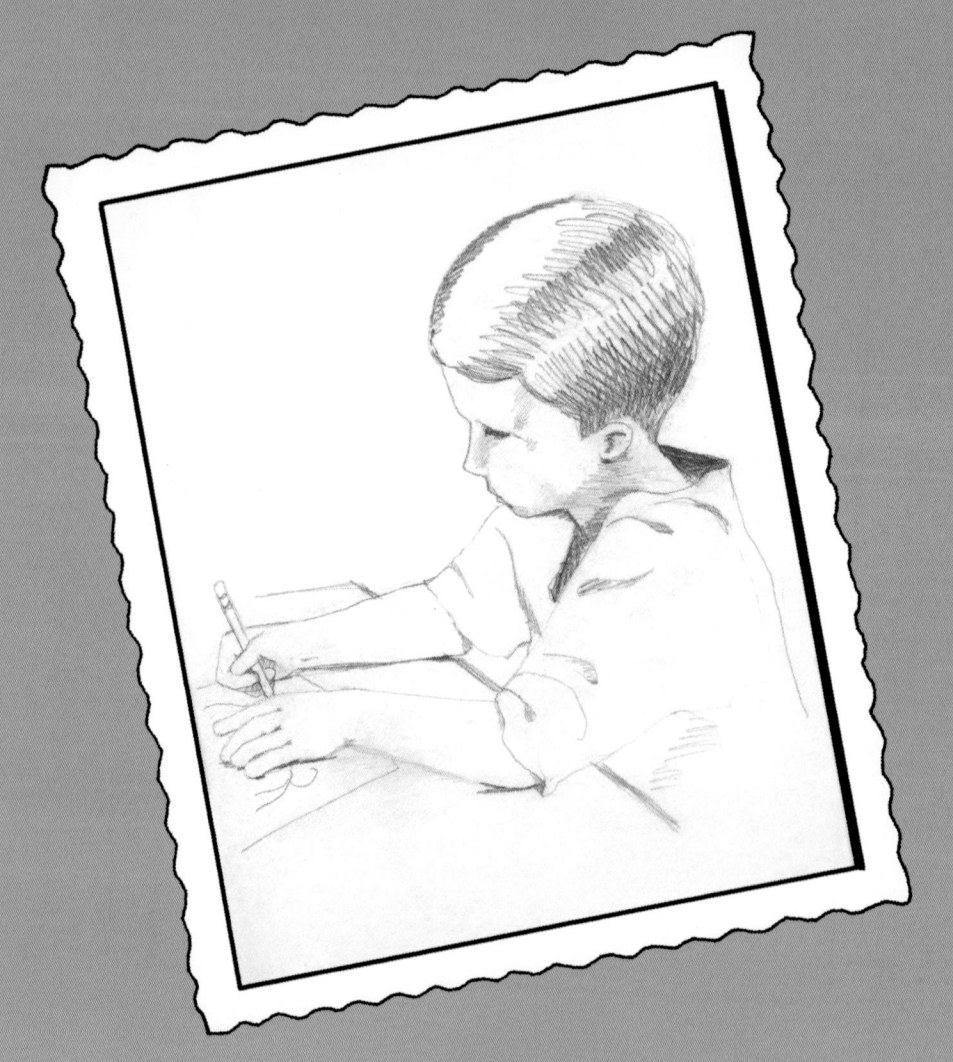

It surely wasn't learned.

Let's nurture it and give him time,

so he'll get what he yearns.

Your child is not special;

he doesn't get straight A's.

How can he be gifted?

It seems he's in a daze.

He's always
    asking questions,

but his homework's
        never done.

It's not fair he gets a special class

'cause he's having too much fun.

All children should be special.

They all have different needs.

Why do we provide for some,

yet halt some others' dreams?

All the other parents

can say what's on their mind

to get their children
what they need.

Please don't
leave me behind!